HOW IS CHRISTIANITY DIFFERENT FROM OTHER RELIGIONS?

CONTENDERS BIBLE STUDY SERIES™

JOHN ANKERBERG
DILLON BURROUGHS

Advancing the Ministries of the Gospel
AMG *Publishers*

God's Word to you is our highest calling.

Contenders Bible Study Series

How Is Christianity Different from Other Religions?

First Printing, May 2008
ISBN 13: 978-089957-780-7

Editing by Rick Steele and Christy Graeber

Layout by PerfecType, Nashville, Tennessee

Cover Design by Indoor Graphics Corp., Chattanooga, Tennessee

Printed in Canada
13 12 11 10 09 08 –T– 6 5 4 3 2 1

Table of Contents

Session 6:

Foreword

By Dr. Norman Geisler

When Jude wrote his New Testament letter to Christians in the early church he felt compelled to urge his readers to "contend for the faith" (Jude 1:3). His words continue to provide a strong motivation for us today to understand the reasons behind what we believe both for our own personal growth and in order to communicate our faith to others.

The Contenders series of Bible study books by John Ankerberg and Dillon Burroughs is designed to provide a response for this tremendous need. As followers of Christ, we are instructed to be prepared to share the reason for our hope (1 Peter 3:15). In addition, those still seeking the truth regarding Jesus and the Word of God are encouraged, as the hearers of Paul in Berea were, to examine the Scriptures to discover if what they had been taught was true (Acts 17:11).

The innovative material found in this series can assist you in two specific ways. First, if you are already a believer in Christ, this series can provide answers to many of the complex questions you may be facing—or that you are asking yourself. Second, if you are a skeptic or seeker of spiritual truth contemplating what it means to follow Jesus Christ, this series can also help provide a factual basis for the Christian faith and the questions in your quest. You can feel free to wrestle with the difficult issues of the Christian faith in the context of friendly conversation with others. This is a powerful tool for individuals who sincerely desire to learn more about God and the amazing truths given to us in the Bible.

If you are one of the people who have chosen to participate in this new series, I applaud your efforts to grow in spiritual truth. Let the pages of this resource provide the basis for your journey as you learn more about contending for the faith we communicate in Jesus Christ.

Dr. Norman Geisler,
co-founder of Southern Evangelical Seminary
and author of seventy books, including the award-winning
Baker Encyclopedia of Christian Apologetics

Introduction

Welcome to the Contenders series! This small-group curriculum was developed with the conviction that claims about today's spiritual issues can and should be investigated. Christianity, sometimes stereotyped as non-intellectual and uneducated, is not allowed to make assertions of faith without providing practical answers why it should be taken seriously. If the Bible claims to be God's Word and claims to provide explanations for the most significant issues of life, both now and eternally, these assertions should be carefully examined. If this investigation proves these beliefs flawed, the only reasonable choice is to refuse to follow the Christian Scriptures as truth. However, if our investigation of the evidence leads to the discovery of truth, then the search will have been worthwhile. In fact, it will be life-changing.

Christians understand that God welcomes sincere seekers of truth. In fact, Jesus Christ Himself openly cheered such inquiry. The Bible is not a book shrouded in mystery, open to only a select group of experts. It is widely available for discussion and learning by anyone. The core beliefs of Christianity are publicly presented to anyone willing to consider their truths, whether skeptic, seeker, or life-long believer.

Consider this book your invitation. Investigate the choices, analyze the beliefs, and make your decisions. But be prepared—the truth you encounter is not another file to simply add to your collection. The truth of God's Word will transform every area of your life.

We often learn that we have mistakenly believed something that turns out to be false. We may even find ourselves not wanting to accept truth because it infringes upon our lifestyle or conflicts with long-held personal values. Through this series of discussion questions we will journey together to answer the question Pilate asked Jesus long ago: "What is truth?" (John 18:38). As authors, it is our hope that you will ultimately come to realize that Christian faith is based upon solid evidence worthy to build one's life upon. Whether you are currently still building your opinions on spiritual issues or are already a follower of Christ developing answers for your own questions and the questions of others, these guides will assist you on a captivating exploration of spiritual issues necessary in order to "contend for the faith" (Jude 3).

The Contenders Series for Your Group

The Contenders series is purposely designed to give truth seekers (those still investigating a relationship with Christ) an opportunity to ask questions and probe into the basics of Christianity within the friendly, caring environment of small-group discussion—typically in a group no larger than about a dozen people, with one or two individuals who serve as the discussion leaders. These leaders are responsible to coordinate the regular gatherings, build relationships with group members, and prepare to ask and answer questions, involving each person in the discussion. Through a combination of caring friendships, intelligent conversations, and genuine spiritual interest, it is our hope that these discussions will provide the basis for a fresh approach to exploring key concepts of Christian belief.

Because one of the intentions of this series is to address the real questions of the spiritual seeker, the questions are presented to represent the viewpoints of both the Christian and the skeptic. While the truths of Christianity are explicitly affirmed, hopefully many who join these discussions will find their own viewpoints understood and represented along the way. As seekers and skeptics feel valued in their current beliefs, they will be more open to honest discussion that leads to truth. The ultimate hope behind the Contenders series is that many who are seeking will come to know the truth about Christ, and that those who already follow Jesus will understand how to address the issues of their friends who are still exploring Christianity.

Of course, it is also important that those who already follow Jesus learn to grow in the basic beliefs of the Christian faith. As they do so, it will become easier to communicate the good news of the Christian faith in normal, everyday conversations with co-workers, neighbors, classmates, relatives, and even complete strangers. The process of struggling through these important issues and difficult questions will not only enhance one's own personal growth but also provide many specific details that can be used in everyday scenarios when the topic of faith arises with others.

Many groups will consist of some blend of believers and seekers. For example, your church may use this material for one of its small groups that consists mostly of people who already follow Christ. However, in the process, group members should feel comfortable and even encouraged to invite friends who have yet to begin a relationship with Christ. Special events designed to invite friends from outside of your current group, including simple social opportunities like dinner parties, a game night, movie night, or other activity should be considered. Regardless of the specific options selected, we pray that you will benefit tremendously as you use these guides to connect through interactive discussions about the issues of ultimate importance.

How to Use This Guide

Getting Started

At the start of each session is a segment of introductory material, typically several paragraphs in length. Each participant will want to read this information before the session begins, even if it is read again when the group is together. This "Getting Started" section is written with the skeptic in mind, often including very controversial perspectives to stimulate challenging discussion. As a result, each person should instantly feel the ability to share his or her viewpoint within the safe context of a caring group of friends.

Talk about It

Next, each session includes a range of ten to twenty questions your group can use during discussion. Most groups will find it impossible to use every single question every time. The options are either to choose which questions best fit the needs of your group, or to use the questions for more than one time together. The key component of this "Talk about It" section is to include each and every person, allowing the conversation to help people process their thoughts on the issue.

Often, the opening question of each session is a simple opinion question. Through the use of this ice-breaker approach, the conversation quickly takes off as each person offers his or her thoughts on a non-threatening issue that touches on the topic of the particular session. Certainly, the creativity of the group may also provide additional or alternative ice-breaker questions or activities to start each session. The goal is to achieve quick and enjoyable involvement by everyone in the group.

Here's What I'm Thinking

The next section, called "Here's What I'm Thinking," transitions the time of discussion toward a more emotional element. The questions in this section deal directly with personal responses to the material in each session rather than just intellectual facts or opinions. This is a time to communicate what each person is feeling about the topic, since this is a critical step in helping a person come to a personal decision about the issue.

What Now?

In the "What Now?" section, participants are challenged to move beyond both intellectual and emotional responses toward personal application of the material shared in the session. Once each person has considered his or her personal position on the issue, the next part of the process is to determine how this position influences daily living. One interesting impact of this section is that each person will begin to understand the implications of both true and faulty beliefs, along with charting personal changes in belief formation from one session to the next.

Consider This

Each session also includes one or more segments called "Consider This," designed to provide additional factual material appropriate to each discussion. Each "Consider This" section is immediately followed by a question based on the material, so it's important (especially for leaders) to read and understand this part before each meeting.

What Others Have Said

Throughout each session, participants will discover various quotes on the topic of discussion. Rather than quoting primarily academic sources, these quotes provide diverse perspectives from those critical of the Christian faith and well-known personalities from today's culture, along with well-worded thoughts from some of today's top writers.

Additional Resources

At the end of each guide, we have provided a list of several resources from the authors on the issue. This is only an introduction to a vast array of print, audio, video, and electronic materials based on decades of research in these areas.

A Word to Discussion Leaders

One distinctive feature of the Contenders series is that the learning does not end with the material found in this book. The series website www.contendersseries.com is loaded with interactive links to numerous online articles, outside internet links, video clips, audio responses, and creative ways to help direct the discussions in your group. We hope you'll also find it to be an excellent personal study source as well. And if you still don't find the answer you're looking for, or just want to connect with the authors of this resource, you'll find a place where you can email your questions and other feedback for personal responses.

Creating Boundaries

These guides consist mostly of questions for one reason—they are intended to spark conversation rather than fill-in-the-blank answers. In one sense, these discussions are not conventional Bible studies, though they often refer to Bible verses and biblical themes. Instead, consider these sessions as study guides, designed to assist participants in discussing what they feel and think on important spiritual issues.

Each topic is developed around a central point and clear conclusion, but they leave much of the "middle" open to the thoughts of those involved in the discussion. Every person brings perspectives, past experiences, and personal questions to the group. Rather than suppress these individual contributions, each session seeks to draw out the thoughts of each person, comparing the thinking of those in the group with what the Bible communicates in order to point members toward spiritual growth.

Much of the group's success will be determined by its leader(s). Those coordinating the group can also find additional material for each session at the Contenders series website at www.contendersseries.com. At the website, leader(s) will find suggested articles, additional facts, and suggested answers for many of the questions in each session. (Individual participants in your group are welcome to use these resources as well.) In addition, a personal daily study in the AMG Following God™ series called *Defending Your Faith* is available for those who desire a more in-depth study that can be used in combination or separately from these group guides.

In addition, you may want to keep the following list of suggestions in mind as you prepare to participate in your group discussions.[1]

1. The Contenders series does not require that the topics be discussed in an exact order. The guides, in addition to the topics within each guide, can be utilized in any order or even independently of each other, based on the needs of your group or class.

2. It is important to read over the material before each meeting (especially for leaders). The more familiar you are with the topic, the better your ability to discuss the issue during the actual group experience.

3. Actively participate in group discussion. The leader of this group is not expected to share a lecture, but to encourage each person to share in dialogue. This

includes both points of agreement and disagreement. Plan to share your beliefs openly and honestly.

4. Be sensitive to other people in the group. Listen attentively when others share and affirm whenever possible. It is important to show respect for the opinions of others even if they don't agree with your position. However, it is likewise important to affirm the biblical truths of each topic in wrapping up each area of discussion.

5. Be careful not to dominate the conversation. Feel free to share, but be sensitive to the length of time that you share in relation to the input of others in the group.

6. Stay focused on the discussion topic. Discussion can easily digress into side topics that may be equally important, but are unrelated to the session in discussion. As a leader, feel free to say: "That's a good issue to discuss. We should talk about that more sometime, but we need to get back to the topic for this session."

7. Encourage group participants to bring a Bible with them. While we believe there is no "perfect" Bible translation, we believe it is important to be sensitive to the needs of seekers and newer believers in your group by at least including a contemporary translation such as the New International Version or New Living Translation that can help provide quick understanding of Bible passages. Many good study Bibles with helpful notes are also available today to help group members in their growth. In these guides, the New International Version has been used unless otherwise noted.

8. Invest some extra time reading in the Bible, other recommended resources, or related audio and video content as you work through these sessions. The "Additional Resources" section at the back of each guide provides several such resources to enhance your growth.

The Greatest of These Is Love

Christianity is all about Christ. The very Son of God left the glory of heaven, was born of a woman, lived among ordinary people like you and me, and died a horrific death, before His resurrection and ascension back to heaven. Shortly before His death, He shared with His followers, "Greater love has no man than this, that he lay down his life for his friends" (John 15:13). Jesus provided a perfect example of this love by offering His life for us. As the apostle Paul later wrote, "Now these three remain: faith, hope, and love. But the greatest of these is love" (1 Corinthians 13:13).

As we learn to "contend for the faith," it is of utmost importance that we live with this same overwhelming love to those we encounter. The Christian faith provides more than ample evidence for the hope that we have in Christ. We invite you to explore these life-changing truths with others in a small-group context that leads to even further growth in your spiritual journey. May God bless you as you pursue the truth of Christ and "contend for the faith."

Setting the Stage: How Is Christianity Different from Other Religions?

According to the website Adherents.com, the following are the ten largest world religions practiced today:

Top Ten Major World Religions Ranked by Size	
Christianity	2.1 billion
Islam	1.3 billion
Secular/Nonreligious/Agnostic/Atheist	1.1 billion
Hinduism	900 million
Chinese traditional religion	394 million
Buddhism	376 million
Primal-Indigenous religions	300 million
African Traditional religions	100 million
Sikhism	23 million
Juche	19 million

Source: http://www.adherents.com/Religions_By_Adherents.html

Christianity (in all forms) represents approximately one-third of the world's population. Yet this still excludes well over four billion people. According to Christian teaching, all of these other religions are wrong and separate themselves from the one true God. How can one religion be so narrow-minded and exclusive?

Are Christians really so arrogant that they believe all of these people will miss out on heaven just because they didn't happen to do the "church thing"? Many of these people have not even heard about Jesus or had an opportunity to follow the Bible's teachings. Even if they did, many live in cultures where they would be shunned by their families or face other hardships for believing in a religion foreign to their local culture. Will these people all really be held responsible for not choosing to believe in Jesus? Will all of the people we have ever met who are Buddhist, Muslim, Hindu, or agnostic "pay for it" in the afterlife with an eternity of suffering?

Even some Christian leaders have now adopted views that are more accepting of our global cultures. Some now suggest that as long as a person believes in an ultimate God and tries to please Him, that this is enough. Others have gone further and believe that everyone goes to heaven. In the view of these individuals, it is inconsistent that a loving God would send anyone into an eternal hell. To them, it simply makes more sense to accept that everyone will be with God forever after life on this earth is complete.

Is the road that leads to heaven really narrow, or is it more like a multi-lane interstate highway? If other religions are teaching their followers to perform acts of kindness, help the poor, and promote peace, then why wouldn't God accept them? Aren't we really all praying to the same God, whether we address this higher power as Allah, Yahweh, Jesus, or we communicate with the spirits in Eastern religions?

In this series of discussions, we'll examine what some of the major world religions teach and compare each with the beliefs of Christianity. As part of our time together, we'll also investigate what Mormons and Jehovah's Witnesses believe, since they are often labeled "Christian," yet hold several beliefs that are distinct from traditional Christianity. Throughout these discussions, you will have the opportunity to examine what other religions claim and to determine whether they all teach the same basic message and communicate with the same God, or whether the difference leads to different conclusions.

Is Jesus "the way" or only one of many ways to God? Does God reject the millions of people who follow other religious traditions? Are followers of many of today's religions really talking to the same God and teaching the same basic beliefs? Get prepared for some lively conversations as we investigate the differences between Christianity and other religions.

Don't All Religions Teach the Same Basic Beliefs?

Getting Started

In a 2006 interview on CNN's *Larry King Live*, actor George Clooney was asked about the issue of faith in his life:

> In talking about religion, if you're well known, anything you say, it sort of ticks off a bunch of other people and attacks their belief. So I always try to say that, you know, first and foremost, that whatever anybody believes as long as it doesn't hurt anybody else, it's fair enough, and works, and I think, is real, and matters. I don't happen to have those beliefs, as much, you know, I don't believe in those things.[2]

His perspective mirrors the attitudes of millions of others who react to questions about spirituality with the answer, "Whatever you believe is okay as long as it doesn't hurt anyone else." As Dr. Harvey Cox, a professor at Harvard Divinity School, wrote: "More and more people view the world's religious traditions as a buffet from which they can pick and choose."[3] But how authentic is such thinking?

In our politically-correct world, is the traditional teaching of Christianity, that all non-Christians are misguided and go to hell after death, still an accurate belief? A growing number of people today believe that many of today's religions teach the same basic beliefs regarding morality and good deeds. Does it really matter if the god is named Buddha, Allah, or Jesus if faith in that deity results in a moral life that helps other people?

What does it matter to God about the name we give Him or the way we choose to follow Him? Isn't it tough enough to live a life of integrity without worrying whether a person attends a church, a synagogue, or a mosque? Who really cares whether the "right" holy day is Friday, Saturday, Sunday, or all three (That would make for a nice three-day weekend tradition!)? To many, it's not God that seems so picky; it's the various groups of people who follow Him. It seems there are as many views of God as there are people. Surely there are more ways than one to reach God.

What if George Bernard Shaw had it right when he said, "There is only one religion, though there are a hundred versions of it."[4]? What if the old tale is correct, that God is like an onion: as we peel back the layers, we see different aspects of who He is, but it is still the same onion, no matter how we slice it? Certainly all religions have part of the truth, but should any particular religion, including Christianity, claim to have the truth wrapped up in a pretty box? This is a pretty narrow view—or is it?

Talk about It

1. In your opinion, what are some of the reasons there are so many gods and religions in the world today?

2. Why do people claim that many of today's world religions really hold the same basic teachings? What evidence is often given as their support?

3. What do you think of the statement, "Whatever you believe is okay as long as it doesn't hurt anyone else"? What reasons can you provide as an explanation for your answer?

4. What information would you need to persuade you that two different religions hold contradictory views about God?

Here's What I'm Thinking

Are We All Praying to the Same God?

During the days following the catastrophic terrorist events of September 11, 2001, President George W. Bush called for a national day of prayer. He urged people of all faiths to pray for America. Interfaith religious services were televised from the National Cathedral in Washington, D.C. and from Yankee Stadium in New York. These services included clerics from Judaism, Christianity, Islam, Buddhism, and Hinduism. They offered prayers to God collectively, addressing Him as "the God of Abraham, the God of Muhammad, and the Father of Jesus Christ." Popular television personality Oprah Winfrey led the service held in New York City and boldly declared that all people pray to the same God.

Is Oprah right? Do Jews, Christians, Muslims, and Hindus worship the same God? If so, people of all faiths can live peaceably in this world, can't they?

Religious pluralism is the view that all religions, certainly all major or ethical religions, are equally valid paths to God or to ultimate reality. For the pluralist, *many* religious roads lead to God and salvation. And yet, given the present cultural milieu of globalism, multiculturalism, relativism (in both truth and morality), and especially the postmodern spirit, the growing climate of religious pluralism poses a serious challenge to the integrity of the Christian faith.[5]

5. How do you feel about the statement that "all people pray to the same God"? Do you agree with this conclusion? Why or why not?

6. Does it seem reasonable that all religions can be true despite significant differences in their beliefs? Why or why not?

7. Many think that people should be accepting of all religions. What is the difference between tolerance and acceptance of a religion?

Isn't It Narrow-Minded to Claim Only One Religion Has the Truth?

Christianity does not claim that there is no truth to be found outside of the Bible. It only claims that the Bible is true and that whatever is contradictory to the Bible is false. As Dr. Norman Geisler writes:

> There is much that is good and true in non-Christian religions. For example, Confucius said, "Do not do to others what you would not have them do to you"—sometimes called the negative Golden Rule. This is not contradictory to the positive Golden Rule of Jesus: "Do to others what you would have them do to you, for this sums up the Law and the Prophets" (Matthew 7:12). Also, Buddhism and most other religions are in harmony with Christianity in teaching that we should respect our parents and that murder is wrong. Christianity does not teach that only the Bible contains truth. It

only affirms that the Bible is true and that
everything that contradicts it is false. . . .[6]

Christianity is indeed exclusive—it claims that only those
who believe in Christ will find salvation—but it is not narrow-
minded, intolerant, or bigoted. *People* can be broad-minded
or narrow-minded but not in regards to *ideas*. Ideas are not
broad or narrow; they are true or false. The claim that Christ
is the only way to salvation is either true or false.

8. What do you think of the idea that if God is all
    loving, He would give us only one way to heaven and
    mark it clearly with evidence? Does this come across
    as arrogant or simply accurate? Why or why not?

9. How can an overly-narrow approach toward other
    religions hurt Christians who desire to share their
    faith with those of other religions?

What Are Some Examples That Other Religions Hold to Different Teaching, from One Another?

The *Bhagavad Gita* states: "Howsoever men may approach
me, even so do I accept them; for, on all sides, whatever path

they may choose is mine" (*Bhagavad Gita* 4:11). Do different religions really worship the same God? Although this may sound like an appealing option in our culture, the main difficulty with this position is that the major world religions teach conflicting views on many major issues. For example, the following chart reveals what the founders of some of today's religions teach about the nature of God:[7]

Krishna	Mix of polytheism (many gods) and impersonal pantheism (all is God). The universe is eternal.
Zoroaster	One good god and one evil god (religious dualism).
Buddha	Essentially taught agnosticism; some would even say atheism. God is not relevant.
Muhammad	One personal God who cannot have a son.
Jesus Christ	One personal God who does have a Son.
Joseph Smith (founder of Mormonism)	Essentially polytheistic. Taught that there are many gods and that the Father of Christ has a human body.
Baha'u'llah (of the Bahai faith)	God and the universe, which is an emanation of God, are co-eternal.

Source: http://www.spotlightministries.org.uk/plural.htm

Another significant difference is regarding how various religions view Jesus Christ. For example, in Christianity, Jesus is the only Son of God and the way, the truth, and the life (John 14:6). However, according to Judaism, Jesus is not God's

Son or Messiah. Jesus is one **of three gods** in Mormonism, a created being according to Jehovah's Witnesses, and a mere prophet who did not die on a cross according to Islam. Contrasting views abound in other areas as well, revealing that the beliefs and teachings of major religions hold more differences than similarities.

10. In light of the above differences, why do many people continue to claim all (or many) religions hold the same or similar beliefs?

11. If religions are so different, why do you think God allows all of them to exist?

12. Since religions have so many differences, do you think there is any way one particular religion can have the correct version of the truth? Why or why not?

13. Do you think it is judgmental to tell someone of another religion that his or her beliefs are wrong? Why or why not?

What Now?

14. How do you feel about Christianity's claims to be the only way to God? Does this bother you or not?

15. What are some ways we can discuss Christianity with those in other religions in a respectful manner? Do you think it is compromise of the Christian faith to talk with other people about their religion? Why or why not?

Consider This

In this session we will investigate how other religions compare with Christianity. Concerning the discussion questions, you are not expected to have all of the answers. As authors, all we ask is that you have an open viewpoint and a desire to learn.

In fact, you are probably involved in a group discussion right now due to your curiosity to discover answers regarding some of your own doubts, or at least the doubts of others in your life. Rather than pretending to have the issues all figured out, feel free to express some of your difficult questions and concerns as you continue with your group. The only way to find the answers to your questions is to ask the real questions that still exist in your own mind.

To help identify ways your viewpoints or beliefs are growing during these sessions, throughout this series you will have opportunities to express where you currently stand on this journey. As you continue to learn, you may find some of your opinions changing from one session to the next. The key idea to remember is that this is a time of growth rather than a test. The more time you invest seeking the truth regarding God and His plans for our lives, the better your understanding will become on the issues discussed in this guide.

16. Mark the following statement out of each pair below that best describes your opinion regarding other religions:

___ It is important to talk with people of other religions in order to tell them about Jesus.
___ We don't need to understand other religions; we just need to tell people about the teachings of Christianity.

___ Studying other religions is likely to lead people away from Christianity.
___ Studying other religions can help us better understand others and help us live out the Christian faith.

___ I really struggle to share what I believe with other people.

___ Talking about my spiritual beliefs comes naturally to me.

___ I would like to know more about other religions to help communicate my Christian faith effectively.

___ I am more concerned about understanding other religions for my own personal growth.

SESSION 1

What's So Unique about Christianity?

Getting Started

Today's choices are sometimes overwhelming. Starbucks™ offers over twenty thousand different combinations of coffee drinks. When you stop to buy orange juice at your local market, you can now choose from organic, regular, with or without calcium, some pulp, lots of pulp, no pulp, and extra vitamin fortified.

Have you tried to choose a tube of toothpaste lately? There are dozens of choices at most stores, ranging from herbal, added fluoride, baking soda, original formula, various children's selections with every cartoon character from today's shows, and a multitude of colors, sizes, and other assorted options. One consumer shared:

> About 10 years ago, I went to the Gap to buy a pair of jeans. I tend to wear my jeans until they're falling apart, so it had been a while since

my last purchase. A nice young saleswoman greeted me.

"I want a pair of jeans—32-28," I said.

"Do you want them slim fit, easy fit, relaxed fit, baggy or extra baggy?" she replied. "Do you want them stone-washed, acid-washed or distressed? Do you want them button-fly or zipper-fly? Faded or regular?"

I was stunned. I sputtered out something like, "I just want regular jeans. You know, the kind that used to be the only kind."

The trouble was that there was no such thing as "regular" jeans anymore. Besides, with all these options before me, I was no longer sure that I wanted "regular" jeans. Perhaps the easy fit or the relaxed fit would be more comfortable. So I decided to try them all.[8]

Choices have given American consumers so many options that some experts have begun to question how helpful these choices actually are. One noted psychologist has suggested, "There's a point where all of this choice starts to be not only unproductive, but counterproductive—a source of pain, regret, worry about missed opportunities and unrealistically high expectations." In fact, some researchers find that too much choice can actually lead people to take less positive risks in making selections and to use simplifying strategies in place of more considered choices.[9]

With such an overwhelming number of choices in every area of life, ranging from the groceries we buy to the type of car we drive, how can a person ever be expected to become knowledgeable enough to select the best option of anything? In the end, how much of a difference is there between many of these choices anyway? Is it really a matter of one choice being better than the other, or is it simply a matter of personal preference? It seems like there are few categories of products where there is one "right" choice for everyone.

"Careful examination of the basic tenets of the various religious traditions demonstrates that, far from teaching the same thing, the major religions have radically different perspectives on the religious ultimate." —Harold A. Netland[10]

Is the same true with choosing a religion? Is religion simply a matter of preference? Should we even try to figure out which religion is best? To many, today's religions seem pretty much the same. Is it simply a matter of what works best for each person? If so, does it really matter which religion we choose to follow or whether we choose one at all?

Talk about It

1. Do you have a friend, coworker, or classmate of another religion? What have you noticed that is different about his or her religious practices?

2. How would you respond if someone asked you what you knew about the following world religions?
- Judaism
- Islam
- Hinduism
- Buddhism

3. What do you think are some of the reasons a person would switch from one religion to another?

Here's What I'm Thinking

Basic Differences in Major World Religions

➤ Buddhism

- Teaches that there is no personal god.
- Presents a view of life as one big cycle of reincarnation filled with pain, largely because life is characterized by impermanence.
- Claims ignorance, rather than sin, is the roadblock to spiritual insights.
- Its doctrine is summed up in the Four Noble Truths: 1) Life is basically suffering; 2) the origin of that suffering lies in craving or grasping; 3) the end of suffering is possible through the ending of craving; and 4) the way to end craving and to escape continual rebirth is by following Buddhist practice, known as the Noble Eightfold Path.

➤ *Hinduism*

- Adherents believe in millions of gods or incarnations of gods that can be worshiped.
- Teaches the physical universe is not the creation of a personal God but a sort of unconscious extension of the divine. It is: 1) without beginning, and some would say endless, and 2) an illusion, because the only true reality is Brahman (the spiritual essence of all).
- The ultimate goal of salvation in Hinduism is escape from the endless cycle of birth, death, and rebirth to join with Braman.
- Four *yogas,* or ways of reaching such salvation, are described: (1) *Jnana yoga,* the way of knowledge, employs philosophy and the mind to comprehend the unreal nature of the universe; (2) *Bhakti yoga,* the way of devotion or love, works for salvation through the emotional worship of a divine being; (3) *Karma yoga,* the way of action, strives toward salvation by performing works without regard for personal gain; and (4) *Raja yoga,* "the royal road," makes use of meditative yoga techniques. *Raja yoga* is usually viewed as the highest way. However, for the majority of people who cannot become wandering monks, the other ways are considered valid.
- Most Hindus believe that they have many incarnations ahead of them before they can find final salvation, although some sects believe that a gracious deity may carry them along the way more quickly.

➤ *Islam*

- Adherents follow Allah as God and believe that Muhammad is His prophet.

- The Qu'ran is the book of ultimate authority.
- Teaches that salvation is dependent on a person's actions and attitudes. However, *tauba* ("repentance") can help quickly turn an evil person toward the virtue that will save him. Islam does not hold out the possibility of salvation through the work of God on the behalf of people, but invites people to accept God's guidance as to what people should do.
- Acts of worship in Islam are embodied in the Five Pillars: 1) A Muslim must recite the basic creed, "There is no God but Allah, and Muhammad is His Prophet"; 2) recite prayers of praise to Allah five times daily while facing Mecca; 3) give money to the poor; 4) fast for one month a year (daytime only); and 5) make a pilgrimage at least once to Mecca, the city where Allah revealed the Qu'ran to Muhammad.
- The final judgment day is described in remarkable terms. On that last day every person will account for what he has done and be weighed in the scales of Allah. A person's works throughout life must be more good than bad. Eternal existence will be determined on the basis of those actions.

➢ *Christianity*

- Adherents believe in one God who exists in three persons (Father, Son, and Spirit).
- Teaches that people are born with a nature that is inclined to sin and do wrong.
- Teaches that Jesus is God's one and only Son, the second person of the Trinity, who came to live on Earth in human form, being fully God and fully man. He died on the cross to pay for the sins of all people, rose three days later, and continues to live today.

- Proclaims there will be a final day of judgment for all people. Each person will be fairly judged regarding their thoughts and actions according to God's standards. Traditional Christian doctrine asserts that those who have not believed in Jesus in this life will spend eternity in hell, while those who did believe in Jesus by faith are forgiven and spend eternity in heaven.[11]

4. What are some of the major differences you notice about the world religions listed above? How significant do you think these differences are?

5. In your opinion, is it truthful to say that these major world religions are all teaching the same basic truths or an uninformed statement? What reasons can you give for this choice?

The Jesus of Islam and the Jesus of Christianity

Some who claim that all religions are basically the same do not realize the fundamental differences that exist between religions in their most essential beliefs. For instance, in

Christianity, Jesus is God's Son, the second person of the Trinity, and the only means of salvation. Yet Jesus is viewed much differently in other religions. The following chart illustrates some of the major differences regarding belief about Jesus in Islam and Christianity:

Comparing Jesus in Islam and Christianity			
Muslim Jesus	Sura	Biblical Jesus	Verses
Jesus was created	3:59	Jesus is eternal	Micah 5:2
Jesus was human	3:59	Jesus is human and divine	John 1:3
Jesus was not crucified	4:157	Jesus died on the cross for our sins	John 1:29
The five pillars provide salvation	9:20–22; 4:124	Jesus alone provides salvation	Acts 4:12
Jesus did not die, therefore he did not resurrect	4:157	Jesus rose from the dead and is now living	John 11:25
Jesus is not to be worshiped	5:75	Jesus is to be worshiped	Philippians 2:11
Jesus was just another prophet	2:136; 2:84	Jesus is God	Mark 14:61–62

6. Do you think a person could realistically follow either Islam or Christianity and not experience any major differences? Why or why not?

7. What do you think are some of the most significant differences between the two views of Jesus illustrated above?

What Happens in the End?

Another major sticking point among world religions is the belief in the afterlife. The following describes the major viewpoints of the afterlife in some of today's world religions:

Agnosticism	Not sure there is one.
Atheism	We simply cease to exist.
Buddhism	Reincarnations until one reaches nirvana.
Christianity	In heaven with God for eternity or in hell separated from God for eternity.
Hinduism	Absorption into the universe after a series of reincarnations.
Islam	"Soul sleep" until Judgment Day, then Paradise or hell.
Judaism	Whatever God provides (not clear).

The Christian view of the afterlife is distinctive in many respects. It teaches that death is not merely an illusion, or eternal extinction, or an inevitable door to heaven or the next life, or multiple lives (reincarnation). Further, it claims that heaven is not merely a positive experience in life, or a higher state of consciousness. Hell is not a negative condition in life, or a temporary purgatory, or the consequence of unenlightened consciousness in this life.

Accordingly, death is part of the punishment resulting from the sins of people. According to the Bible, there are only two kinds of death. First, there is physical death, which involves the temporary separation of the spirit from the body. In the resurrection, the body is later rejoined with the human spirit. Second, there is eternal spiritual death, or the eternal separation of the human spirit from God. This condition has no remedy. Death is not good; it has never been good.

> *Physical death*—separation from the body—is not good, since by it man is left "unclothed" in an unnatural state (2 Corinthians 5:4; Philippians 3:21; 1 Corinthians 15:53–54).
>
> *Spiritual death*—separation from God—is not good, since by it one is eternally separated from God. "Death" and "life" are irreconcilable and opposite conditions of existence in both this life and the next. Apart from Christ, death leads to one thing only: eternal judgment (Hebrews 9:27). But with Christ, death leads to life (John 11:25–26).

The Bible teaches that prior to salvation, even as they are alive, all men and women exist in a state of spiritual death or separation from God. Their human spirits are "dead" to those things that God is truly concerned about (Luke 15:24–32; Ephesians 2:1). Even though they are alive physically, they do not consider the one true God, nor do they honor Him or care about His interests. Whatever God or concept of God they may believe in, they do not concern themselves with the concerns of the one true God (Romans 3:10–18).

According to the Bible, physical and spiritual death exists for one reason: sin. God warned Adam and Eve that if they disobeyed Him, in that day they would die (Genesis 2:17). They died first spiritually and then physically. This is why the Bible teaches, "The wages of sin is death" (Romans 6:23). Because sin causes death, the problem of sin must be dealt with before death can be dealt with. As one philosopher has noted, one little sin committed against an infinitely loving God deserves an infinite punishment—which is eternal separation from God in hell forever. Of course, we have all committed more than one sin. This is the reason for the Christian teaching on the atonement: that Christ died for the sins of the world.

Since Christ paid the full penalty of sin (Colossians 2:13), there is no longer the possibility of the believer suffering God's judgment for his sins, which is the "second death." Instead, the believer will join God forever at the point of physical death. This is the essence of the term "saved." And it must be stressed that people must come to belief in the atoning death of Jesus Christ before they die or they cannot be saved. The only condition is to accept what God has done in the person of Christ. Thus, the biblical view is that the saved are with God; that He takes them home to heaven to be with Him at the moment of death (Luke 23:43; John 12:26; Acts 7:59).

The Christian hope, then, is not a view of gradual, spiritual self-progression after death, rather it is Christ's gift to us of physical resurrection and eternal immortality based on His death, resurrection, and life (Romans 4:25; 1 Corinthians 6:14). Those who accept Christ inherit heaven for eternity; those who reject God and His mercy inherit hell for eternity (2 Peter 2:4, 9). There is no possibility of altering one's fate after death (Hebrews 9:27; Luke 16:19–31).

SESSION 2

Death, then, is not extinction, as some religions teach. It does not involve reincarnation, where the soul experiences many lifetimes, as occult religions teach. It does not involve ultimate union with or absorption into some impersonal, divine essence as many Eastern cults teach. Christians, by and large, believe that non-Christians will exist eternally separated from God after they die.

8. Which of these views of the afterlife listed above makes the most sense to you? Which makes the least sense?

9. Why do you think the idea of reincarnation is appealing to so many people today?

10. Why is a religion's view of the afterlife such an important part of its belief system?

What Now?

11. Why do you think people become so emotionally involved when discussing religion? What reasons can you give for this level of concern?

12. How do you feel now about the uniqueness of Christianity?

13. What are one or two aspects of Christianity you could share with someone that will distinguish it from other world religions?

Consider This

14. The biggest difficulty the people I know face about religion is:
    ___ They don't care enough to investigate what they believe.
    ___ They haven't taken the time to consider what they believe.
    ___ They don't understand the differences between the beliefs of major world religions.
    ___ They simply accept what they have been told by their parents.
    Other: _____

15. The biggest struggle I see in studying other religions is that:
    ___ I don't know very much about other religions.
    ___ I don't know people involved in other religions.
    ___ I don't care about other religions.
    ___ I'm still trying to figure out what I believe about my own faith.
    Other: _____

16. My personal view about other religions is that:
    ___ Christianity is unique among the religions of the world.
    ___ Christianity is my religion, but I don't try to change the minds of others.
    ___ Christianity is simply one of many good religions out there.
    Other: _____

Isn't It Enough for a Person to Be Sincere?

Getting Started

"Just try your best."

Have you ever had a parent or teacher encourage you with these words? As children, we are often encouraged even if we can't color inside the lines or draw quite like the picture we are trying to create. But does trying hard or being sincere count when it comes to spiritual matters?

Isn't that how God treats us? Are we His loving children who are simply asked to try our best? He accepts us regardless of what we choose regarding our religious beliefs? He knows we're not perfect. But because He loves us, He takes whatever sincere efforts we give Him without being judgmental about our problem areas. If we're at least trying, isn't that enough? Why would we want to believe in a God who wouldn't accept our sincere efforts? Who would want to follow such a discouraging God?

Some people think it doesn't matter what you believe, as long as you're sincere. Several years ago, someone put cyanide inside new medicine bottles and placed them on store shelves. People bought these bottles and sincerely believed they were what the label proclaimed. But the sincerity of those consuming the pills did not help them, and the end result was death. On the religious front, centuries ago people sincerely believed that the gods at war caused thunder in the sky. We now know that their sincere beliefs were grounded in superstition rather than fact. People can be very sincere in what they believe, but they can also be sincerely wrong.

It's amazing how people often say that sincerity is all you need when it comes to religion, but not to other parts of life. You'd never say this about a historical event such as World War II. You may sincerely believe that Hitler actually won, but you'd be wrong. You could argue the Holocaust never happened, but you would be denying reality.

You'd never apply this kind of thinking to mathematics. No one in his right mind would say that if he sincerely believed hard enough, one plus one would equal three. Could a person sincerely believe that a triangle had four sides and be accepted by others simply because of his sincerity? Why think this way when it comes to spiritual issues?[12]

"Every tiny part of us cries out against the idea of dying, and hopes to live forever." —Ugo Betti

---

It ultimately comes down to "Does God exist?" and if so, "What does he say?" Some people create a God in their own mind who is watching for their next mistake in order to place another mark on their list of sins. Other people believe in a God who accepts them no matter what they do as long as they are sincere. Your view of God determines how you live your life. What really matters is whether God is satisfied by our human efforts or if there is a specific type or object of faith required.

Some would argue that they would not want to believe in or live for a harsh God who expected a particular form of belief. They argue that if God is really loving, He'll take them "as is" without expecting a particular performance in return. But again, is sincerity enough? In this session, we'll discuss this important issue of sincerity as we continue our conversation regarding other religions.

Talk about It

1. Think back to a conversation in which a person came across as uncaring and insincere toward you. How did this make you feel?

2. Why is sincerity such an important part of human relationships?

3. What do you think about the perspective that says that we will go to heaven regardless of what we believe as long as we make a sincere effort? Why do you believe this?

SESSION 3

4. Can a person be sincere but also sincerely wrong? What is an example you have seen of this situation?

Here's What I'm Thinking

Why Sincerity Doesn't Work

What can we say to people who think that sincerity is enough in religion? First, we can point out to them that since sincerity is never enough anywhere else in life, why should it be enough in spiritual matters? For instance, is sincerity enough in medicine, law, finances, or politics? Ask them:

- Do you really believe that it does not matter what a doctor does as long as he or she is sincere?

- Is however a lawyer handles a case acceptable as long as he or she is sincere?

- Is any way a financial manager handles money fine as long as the person is sincere?

- Is any technique okay for a politician as long as he or she is sincere?

- If you got on a bus sincerely thinking you were on your way to New York City, when you actually got on a bus going to California, would your sincerity alter the fact that you were going in the wrong direction?[13]

Sincerity is great, but even more important is the object of your faith. Can't we be sincerely wrong? Of course! Logically speaking, since all religions contradict each other, either one religion or another will be true, but they cannot all be true. But what do we say if we run across someone who says, "I have my truth, and you have your truth. Truth is whatever you want it to be."?

Point out to them that this is inconsistent with how they, or any other person, actually lives. They cannot live what they believe. For example, if their bank took away all their money and said, "We have our truth that you never deposited any money, and you have your truth that you did," this person would be the first to say that we must be objective and rational.

Or look at the tragedy of 9/11. Those who performed those terrible acts of terror sincerely believed what they were doing was a noble act of faith. But would any of those who lost loved ones on that tragic day agree that this was acceptable just because the terrorists involved were sincere? No way!

Still others abide by what Wiccans call the Rede, that "If you harm none, do as you will." But just because you don't hurt another person in the process, does this mean your sincerity is acceptable to God even if you follow a religion inconsistent with what the true God teaches?

According to the Bible, God's plan for us reveals our standing before Him, the consequences of our actions, and the gift of salvation provided by Christ the moment we decide to sincerely trust in Him to save us:

> *Salvation is found in no one else, for there is no other name under heaven given to men by which we must be saved.* (Acts 4:12)

> *Jesus answered, "I am the way and the truth and the life. No one comes to the Father except through me."* (John 14:6)

5. If a person can certainly be sincerely wrong, how
    dangerous can this be when applied to religious
    choices? Does the same principle apply? Why or why
    not?

6. What complaints do people give for the exclusivity of
    Christianity that believes that Jesus is the only way
    to heaven?

The Issue of Truth

If knowing truth is in one's best interest, then the claim of
Christianity to have the truth and the claim of Jesus Christ to
be the truth are worth investigation. Why would those who do
not share our Christian worldview want to consider evaluat-
ing Christianity?

First, it is good to seek truth. The honest search for truth
is one of life's noblest philosophical endeavors. Plato declared,
"Truth is the beginning of every good thing, both in Heaven
and on earth; and he who would be blessed and happy should
be from the first a partaker of the truth." Any religion or
philosophy that makes convincing claims to having absolute
truth is worth consideration because only a few claim this. A
religion that presents solid evidence on behalf of its claim that

it alone is fully true is worth serious consideration for that reason alone. By the way, only Christianity does this.

"Man passes away; generations are but shadows; there is nothing stable but truth."
—Josiah Quincy

Second, the kind of life Christianity offers is one of deep and abundant satisfaction, despite the pain and disappointment we may experience. Jesus claimed He would give us what we really want in life—true meaning and purpose now, and everlasting life in a heavenly existence far beyond our current comprehension. Jesus declared, "I came that they might have life and have it abundantly" (John 10:10) and "I am the resurrection and the life. He who believes in me will live, even though he dies" (John 11:25). He also said, "I am the truth" (John 14:6).

Have you ever had a driver cut you off in traffic and thought, "Hey, that's not right!"? How did you determine that the other driver's action was unfair? In doing so, you were appealing to a higher standard that you expect other drivers to live by. Who gave that standard of right and wrong? Why do all people feel some sense for a need of fairness or justice in the world?

7. Do you believe that there is real, objective truth? What reasons led you to this response?

SESSION 3

8. What would be the implications if there were no such thing as objective, absolute truth? Would it be similar to a city where all of the signal lights were green all of the time? What would be the outcome of such a scenario?

What Can We Learn from Other Religions?

If each religion is different and there is only one true way to God, what good is it to investigate other religions? According to Gerald McDermott, studying other religions can help us understand three key issues:

1. If we are more sensitive to what others believe, we'll be more effective.
2. Learning about other belief systems will help us appreciate our own faith more.
3. Learning from other religions will give us compassion for other people.

Knowing what other people believe will show us that "God is at work in more ways and lands and people that many of us had imagined."[14] God is drawing them to His truths revealed in the Bible. Interestingly, the more we learn about other faiths, the more we feel the need to know more about our own beliefs as well.

9. Which of the three statements listed above do you think is most reflective of your experience of

discussing other religions? Why do you think this is the case?

10. In what ways does talking about the beliefs of other religions motivate you to want to better understand what you personally believe?

Showing Love Regardless of the Differences

The mission organization Frontiers desires to reach Muslim people with the true message of Jesus Christ. As part of their outreach, they have developed a list called "Ten Reasons Why We Love Muslims" that reads:

1. *God loves Muslims!*
   Muslims are loved by God in the same way that He loves all people. Like all humans, Muslims are created in the image of God (Genesis 1:26–27). Like all humans, Muslims sin and fall short of God's glory (Romans 3:23). Like all humans, God loved them so much that He sent His son, so that those who believe in Jesus will have eternal life (John 3:16).
2. *God calls Muslims to Himself!*
   God designed all of us to seek after Him. That includes Muslims. "From one man, he made every nation of men, that they should inhabit the whole earth. . . . God did this so men would seek Him and perhaps reach out to Him and find Him, though He

discussing other religions? Why do you think this is the case?

10. In what ways does talking about the beliefs of other religions motivate you to want to better understand what you personally believe?

Showing Love Regardless of the Differences

The mission organization Frontiers desires to reach Muslim people with the true message of Jesus Christ. As part of their outreach, they have developed a list called "Ten Reasons Why We Love Muslims" that reads:

1. *God loves Muslims!*
   Muslims are loved by God in the same way that He loves all people. Like all humans, Muslims are created in the image of God (Genesis 1:26–27). Like all humans, Muslims sin and fall short of God's glory (Romans 3:23). Like all humans, God loved them so much that He sent His son, so that those who believe in Jesus will have eternal life (John 3:16).
2. *God calls Muslims to Himself!*
   God designed all of us to seek after Him. That includes Muslims. "From one man, he made every nation of men, that they should inhabit the whole earth. . . . God did this so men would seek Him and perhaps reach out to Him and find Him, though He

is not far from each one of us. For in Him we live and move and have our being" (Acts 17:24–31). Like you and I, God has placed "eternity in their hearts" (Ecclesiastes 3:11).

"So little trouble do men take in their search after truth; so readily do they accept whatever comes first to hand." —Thucydides

---

3. *Muslims are our neighbors.*
   Whether in America or in the Middle East, the overwhelming majority of Muslims are peace-loving, hospitable people.
4. *Muslims are people, too!*
   Most Muslims are concerned about the same things as you and I. They want to raise their children well, they are concerned about rising crime and pornography, and work hard to pay their bills and survive. Like us, most Muslims decry human suffering and violence between peoples. Many Muslims yearn for peace, friendship, and a happy life. We share the same concerns and needs.
5. *God is at work among Muslims!*
   Many Muslims are sensitive to God and spiritual things. Because they fear God and are aware of spiritual reality, Muslims often speak of how God appeared to them through dreams and visions, just like he did to the God-fearer Cornelius (Acts 10:1–8). Stories abound of healings because of God's power through Jesus. An increasing number of Muslims are hungry to know about God's dramatic work through Jesus.
6. *Because we are spiritually related.*
   Many Muslims look to 'Ibrahim (Abraham) as "our

forefather" (see Romans 4:1). Since those who follow
Jesus call Abraham "the father of all who believe"
(Romans 4:11), that makes us 'cousins'! Like us,
Muslims believe in one true God, the Creator of all
peoples.

7. *Because they value our Holy Book and Jesus.*
The Qu'ran specifically commends the *Torat* (the first
five books of the Bible); the *Zibur* (the Psalms, or
wisdom literature); and the *injil* (the Gospels). Jesus
was sent by God to earth; Jesus healed many during
His ministry; and He is returning to judge the living
and the dead.

8. *Because they have something to teach us.*
Muslims take the spiritual world very seriously and
generally are more open to discuss spiritual issues.
They have a very high respect for God and His
power. Muslims place a high value on community
and loyalty. Hospitality is very important to them.
These are qualities that most westerners appreciate in
their Muslim friends.

9. *God made promises to their ancestors.*
Many Muslims look to 'Ibrahim (Abraham) as
their ancestor through his first son, Ishmael. God
made this promise to Ibrahim: "As for Ishmael, I
have heard you; behold, I will bless him, and I will
make him fruitful, and I will multiply him. He shall
become the father of twelve princes, and I will make
him a great nation" (Genesis 17:20). God fulfilled
this promise, for there are over one billion Muslims
in the world today!

10. *Because God promised that Muslims who follow
Jesus [i.e., Muslims who have converted to
Christianity] will be part of the multitudes who are
gathered about the Throne of God.*
When God gathers all His people at the end of time,
there will be representatives from every people group

SESSION 3

on the earth, "from every nation and tribe and people and language, standing before the Throne and before the Lamb, clothed in white robes, . . . crying out in a loud voice, 'Salvation to our God who sits on the throne'" (Revelation 7:9–10). (From http://www.frontiers.org/about/reasons.htm).

As a result of their efforts to show the love of Jesus through respect toward Muslim people and culture in areas that do not pertain to sharing the gospel, the Frontier organization has had the opportunity to reach many people in America and across the Muslim world.

11. How do you feel about the approach used by the Frontier organization? Do you think they go too far in adapting to Muslim culture or do you think they have properly adapted their methods to reach those of a different religion? What reasons can you give for your decision?

12. In what ways could the approach used by this mission organization be adapted for your efforts in speaking with someone of another faith?

"For most of us the truth is no longer part of our minds; it has become a special product for experts." —Jacob Bronowski

What Now?

13. Do you feel like you hold insincerity in your own beliefs in any way? What could you do to change in these areas?

14. In what ways does hypocrisy (living differently from what you say you believe) influence what others believe about your faith?

15. In what ways are your own spiritual beliefs based on truth? In what ways are they based on your culture (such as what your parents taught you or where you grew up)?

SESSION 3

16. Do you really believe Jesus told the truth when He said, "I am *the* way, *the* truth, and *the* life" (see John 14:6 [emphasis added])? Why or why not?

Consider This

17. What statements best describe your personal beliefs regarding other religions? (Mark all that apply.)

___ Sincerity is enough when it comes to spiritual beliefs.

___ I don't like that God would not accept someone who is sincere but believes differently than what the Bible teaches.

___ I believe there are objective truths a person must believe in order to know God.

___ It upsets me to think that some of my friends or family who believe differently would not be accepted by God according to the Bible.

___ Some blend of sincerity and truth is what I really believe.

Aren't Mormons and Jehovah's Witnesses Christians?

Getting Started

Combined, there are over 18.6 million Mormons and Jehovah's Witnesses today. Mormonism has exploded at a staggering rate. Over a decade ago, sociologist Rodney Stark calculated that at its rate of growth at that time, membership in the Mormon Church could reach 267 million members worldwide by the year 2080. Since Stark's numbers were published, the movement's growth has accelerated even further.[15] As their numbers have grown, so has their acceptance. In an increasing number of religious studies, these two groups are listed under the broad category of Christianity, creating confusion among people in today's churches.

On a personal level, if you do not already have a friend who is affiliated with one of these groups, you have probably had someone from one of these organizations knock on your door or hand your their literature. At many hotels, you can find the *Book of*

Mormon next to a Bible in your room. Further, in conversations, these individuals say they believe in Jesus and agree with much of what the Bible teaches (or their version of it), but go on to say that in order to know the truth, we must also believe in their teachings.

While these door-knockers are often mocked, insulted, and ridiculed, they continue to produce results. Jehovah's Witnesses, for example, continue to experience a 2.8 percent annual growth rate utilizing this direct approach.

Many of these individuals can share powerful stories of changed lives and behaviors. They are generally extremely friendly and outgoing. It is hard for many to believe that those who work so diligently to share their faith and even talk highly of Jesus would not be accepted as Christians according to what the Bible teaches.

What's the big deal with groups such as Mormons and Jehovah's Witnesses? Is each just another denomination within Christianity or a completely different religion? How are the differences in these groups any different than the differences between Methodists, Baptists, or Presbyterians? Why are Mormons and Jehovah's Witnesses the ones treated as outsiders?

How could a religion based on what Christians call "false teachings" be filled with so many nice people? Didn't the Bible say the world would know we are Christians by our love? Many in these groups are more loving than many Christians based on what we see in daily life. Does this make their teachings acceptable, too?

When it comes down to it, it makes you stop and think. Why is there such controversy about these two groups? Aren't Mormons and Jehovah's Witnesses Christians? Why should they be viewed any differently?

Talk about It

1. What is your initial reaction when you see or encounter a person trying to convert you to Mormonism or the Jehovah's Witnesses?

2. What were the people like that you have met from the Mormon Church or Jehovah's Witnesses?

3. What do you think Mormons and Jehovah's Witnesses have in common with Christianity? What differences have you noticed?

SESSION 4

Here's What I'm Thinking

Just Who Is a Christian?

How do we discern who is a Christian and who is not? While this is difficult at times on a personal level, the Bible provides guidelines defining whether certain teachers or groups are teaching Christian beliefs. In the New Testament, these tests are primarily developed around the person of Christ. Christ's name serves as a fitting acronym for our investigation to define what groups are truly based on the biblical teachings concerning our Lord.

C-Christ: What does the teacher or group say about Jesus? The Bible calls Him God's Son who came in human form, died, and rose from the dead (John 1:1–4).

H-History: What is the background of the person or group? Do they have a reputation of integrity, or is their past suspect or questionable? For instance, if a group predicts the date of Jesus' return or the end of the world and it doesn't happen, it questions their reliability in other areas.

R-Rituals: What is a person required to do? Christianity encourages practices that build maturity in the Christian faith, such as baptism, Bible study, prayer, and gathering together for worship. Non-biblical activities, such as prayers for the dead or rituals based on other religious books, are signs that mark non-Christian movements.

I-Inspiration: What is the person or group's view of the Bible? Is it just a good book to that person or group, or is it the sole source of authority on spiritual issues? Those who add additional books or change the Bible in any way mark themselves as non-Christian movements.

S-Salvation: How does a person know God and enter heaven? The Christian view is that salvation is by grace alone through faith alone in Christ alone. Any works or activities that are required to obtain salvation, mark the person or group as something other than biblical Christianity.

T-Teachers: What is the role of the leaders? The biblical view is that teachers help explain Scripture, but do not add to or take away from it.

4. In what ways do you agree or disagree with the guidelines provided above? What additional information would you add? What would you change?

5. Would you define Mormonism and/or Jehovah's Witnesses as a cult? Why or why not?

6. What comes to mind when you think of a group that is called a cult? Why do you think this is the case?

The Basics of Mormonism and Jehovah's Witnesses

➤ Mormonism
- God: God is a human being who became God.
- Trinity: There are three separate gods, not one.
- Jesus: God's son, but not eternal.

- Bible: The Bible is a good book that was corrupted; the *Book of Mormon* is considered of equal status and as more accurate.
- People and the Afterlife: Humans can become gods.
- Salvation: Faith + works + baptism.

➤ *Jehovah's Witnesses*

- God: There is one God named Jehovah.
- Trinity: There is no Trinity.
- Jesus: He is a created being, Michael the archangel in human form. He was only resurrected spiritually, not physically.
- Bible: The New World Translation of the Bible is the only authorized Bible. It is similar to the King James Version, but includes many theologically-motivated changes to suit their purposes, such as John 1:1–4 (". . . and the Word was a god" rather than "the Word was God").
- People and the Afterlife: Only 144,000 of the most devoted Jehovah's Witnesses will be leaders in heaven. Everyone else will live on a new earth. Unbelievers will be annihilated (cease to exist).
- Salvation: A series of works, including baptism, obedience, learning, and sharing your faith with others.

Based on the above basic beliefs, it is clear that these two groups hold vastly different positions on key Christian teachings. For instance:

- God: In the nature of the one true God there are three persons (Father, Son, and Holy Spirit).
- Trinity: The Trinity is a foundational belief of Christianity.

- Jesus: He is God's only Son, eternal and completely divine and fully human, sinless and perfect in every way. He physically died and physically resurrected Himself from the dead to prove Himself as the Christ.
- Bible: God's inerrant and inspired revelation to humanity. It is our sole authority on matters of faith and practice.
- People and the Afterlife: People are created by God and inherited a sinful nature at birth from Adam and Eve that makes it impossible for anyone (excluding Jesus) to live without committing sins. All people choose to freely sin. After death, all individuals spend eternity in heaven or hell.
- Salvation: Based on God's grace alone received through faith alone in Christ alone, apart from any and all human works.

7. Why do you think so many people believe Mormons and Jehovah's Witnesses are Christians even though they hold completely different beliefs?

8. What are the most surprising differences you noticed in the beliefs of Mormonism and Jehovah's Witnesses listed above?

SESSION 4

9. In your opinion, how can people in these groups hold such different beliefs from Christians and yet often live in ways that seem very "Christian" and moral?

What the Bible Says about False Teachers

The Bible communicates very strong statements regarding false teachers. A few examples include:

> Watch out for false prophets. (Matthew 7:15)

> But there were also false prophets among the people, just as there will be false teachers among you. They will secretly introduce destructive heresies, even denying the sovereign Lord who bought them—bringing swift destruction on themselves. Many will follow their shameful ways and will bring the way of truth into disrepute. In their greed these teachers will exploit you with stories they have made up. Their condemnation has long been hanging over them, and their destruction has not been sleeping. (1 Peter 2:1–3)

> As I urged you when I went into Macedonia, stay there in Ephesus so that you may command certain men not to teach false doctrines any longer nor to devote themselves to myths and endless genealogies. These promote controversies rather than God's

work—which is by faith." (1 Timothy 1:3–4)

*. . . be on your guard so that you may not
be carried away by the error of lawless
men and fall from your secure position.
But grow in the grace and knowledge of
our Lord and Savior Jesus Christ.* (1 Peter
3:17–18)

*Dear friends, although I was very eager to
write to you about the salvation we share, I
felt I had to write and urge you to contend
for the faith that was once for all entrusted
to the saints. For certain men whose
condemnation was written about long ago
have secretly slipped in among you. They are
godless men, who change the grace of our
God into a license for immorality and deny
Jesus Christ our only Sovereign and Lord.*
(Jude 1:3–4)

In light of these warnings, it is critical to evaluate your
own beliefs as well as the beliefs of others. To do so, it is
important to do two things. First, you must learn your own
faith well. This is where personal Bible study, small groups,
classes, church worship gatherings, and Bible study resources
are helpful. It is difficult to compare your beliefs to the beliefs
of others if you do not know what you believe.

Second, you must investigate the beliefs of other religions.
Basing your decision solely on personal appearance or how
nice a person is does not provide an adequate basis of com-
parison with what God communicates in the Bible. Only upon
identifying where a person or group stands on the key issues
of biblical Christianity can we know how they differ from
biblical Christian teachings and use those areas as a bridge to
communicate our faith.

10. If people who hold different beliefs can be sincere, how can we know that sincerity in our own beliefs is any more right than in someone else's beliefs?

11. If Christianity's core beliefs can be traced back directly to Jesus and His apostles, how can Mormons or Jehovah's Witnesses differ so significantly from biblical Christian beliefs?

12. Why do you think the Bible provides such strong warnings against false teachers?

What Now?

13. How would you explain the rapid growth of Mormonism and the Jehovah's Witnesses? Does the fact that these two groups are growing worldwide indicate that their teachings are in some way true? Why or why not?

14. How should Christians act towards people we meet who are involved in Mormonism or the Jehovah's Witnesses? In what ways have past attitudes toward these groups hurt outreach opportunities to these groups today?

15. If you had only five minutes with a person from one of these two groups, how could you help him or her consider the true claims about Jesus found in the Bible?

Consider This

Mark your responses to the following statements based on this discussion. (Mark all that apply.)

16. Who are they...?
   ___ I believe Mormons and Jehovah's Witnesses are Christians.
   ___ Some Mormons and Jehovah's Witnesses are Christians, but not all of them.
   ___ The beliefs of the Mormons and Jehovah's Witnesses are very different from Christianity.

SESSION 4

17. What do they need?

___ I don't think we should try to convert Mormons or Jehovah's Witnesses to Christianity.

___ Mormons and Jehovah's Witnesses need to know how to have a relationship with God based on faith in Jesus Christ like anyone else.

18. How should we relate?

___ Mormons and Jehovah's Witnesses should be completely avoided since they present false teachings.

___ Mormons and Jehovah's Witnesses are people who need to know Christ; therefore, we are called to pray for them, build relationships with them, and communicate the truth about Jesus.

___ Mormons and Jehovah's Witnesses already know about Jesus. We just need to accept them as they are.

Can't a Person Get to Heaven without Jesus?

Getting Started

Today's world offers a membership card for every occasion. At Sears®, there's the Sears credit card. At Speedway®, there's the Speedway pass to save on fuel. Blockbuster® rentals require a membership. American Express® provides special privileges exclusively for members. It seems every company offers a card, membership, password, or special deal designed for exclusive groups of people who have signed up in some way, shape, or form.

Many people look at religion as simply another membership. Similar to membership at a local gym or golf club, a person's religion becomes simply another line on the "memberships" section of the resume. It can be helpful in establishing connections, kind of like meeting someone who was part of your same sorority or fraternity in college, creating a special bond between two people. In a lot of ways, their religious membership fits nicely as another card for their wallet or purse.

When Christianity claims that only Christians go to heaven, people sometimes become vocal in their frustrations. Who would claim to be the only ones with exclusive access privileges to eternity with God? This is not simply an issue of saving ten percent on a purchase or earning frequent flier miles for a discounted flight. The stakes are heaven and hell; who goes and who doesn't. This is about where people will spend eternity.

Jesus was a spiritual leader who focused on love and acceptance, wasn't He? Would He insist that there is only one way to God? If He was really all about unconditional love and complete forgiveness, wouldn't he clear us for access into His kingdom or permit us entrance into someone else's kingdom regardless of what we do in this life? Isn't it enough just to live our lives, try to perform some acts of kindness, and help out people in need once in a while? Certainly God understands, doesn't He?

A heaven for "members only" doesn't sound like much fun anyway. If God really created us, doesn't He love us just the way we are? Why would He change the rules in heaven, granting entrance only to those select few who make the cut for the team? Wouldn't He want everyone there with Him too, apart from the pain and trouble people often face in this world?

Why can't a person get into heaven without Jesus? In this discussion, we'll talk about this important question and try to understand the Bible's perspective on why Jesus is the only way to God. Is God discriminating by not letting everyone into His kingdom, or is there another way to look at this issue?

Talk about It

1. What are some of the ways you have heard people respond when they are told that Jesus is the only way

to God? Why do you think these people reacted this way?

2. From our human perspective, the necessity for some kind of special pass to access heaven can strike us as uncaring or even discriminating. What kind of entry into heaven would people prefer to have?

Here's What I'm Thinking

What the Bible Says about Jesus as the Only Way

> _Salvation is found in no one else_, for there is no other name under heaven given to men by which we must be saved. (Acts 4:12)

> Jesus answered, "I am the way and the truth and the life. _No one_ comes to the Father _except through me_." (John 14:6)

> For **Christ** died for sins once for all, the righteous for the unrighteous, _to bring you to God_. He was put to death in the body but made alive by the Spirit. (1 Peter 3:18)

> Whoever believes _in him_ is not condemned, but whoever does not believe stands

condemned already because he has not believed in the name of God's one and only Son." (John 3:18)

I told you that you would die in your sins; if you do not believe that I am the one I claim to be, you will indeed die in your sins. (John 8:24)

As we have already said, so now I say again: If anybody is preaching to you a gospel other than what you accepted, let him be eternally condemned! (Galatians 1:9)

Now, brothers, I want to remind you of the gospel I preached to you, which you received and on which you have taken your stand. By this gospel you are saved, if you hold firmly to the word I preached to you. Otherwise, you have believed in vain. (1 Corinthians 15:1–2)

And this is the testimony: God has given us eternal life, and this life is in his Son. He who has the Son has life; he who does not have the Son of God does not have life. (1 John 5:11–12)

3. Why do you think the Bible teaches that Jesus is the only way to God?

4. Since the Bible communicates very clearly how a
    person comes to know God and enter heaven, why
    would a person claim that the Bible teaches that
    people go to heaven even if they don't believe in Jesus?

Salvation Rejection

Those who reject the belief that Jesus is the only way to God
often use one of the following excuses or objections as their
reason:

- The majority of the world's population follows non-
  Christian religions. How could so many people be
  wrong? If Jesus is the only way, too many people will
  not go to heaven.
- Christianity is a narrow-minded religion. Any
  religious system that claims to have the "truth"
  cannot be trusted. Christianity cannot be the only
  way.
- Don't other religions offer ways to make it to
  heaven that are just as difficult if not more so than
  in Christianity? How could they be rejected if they
  demand more effort than Christianity?
- How can we know that the Bible's way of entering
  heaven is the right way? Has anyone really proven
  that its teachings are *completely* true?
- What about moral and kind people who do not
  believe in Jesus? Why would they not make it into
  heaven? Some of the nicest people I've met are not

Christians at all. Would God keep them out of heaven anyway?

5. Name some of the assumptions that lie behind the reasons given above. Which of these excuses seems the most reasonable to you? Which seems the most unreasonable?

6. Choose one of the objections listed above and share how you would answer it with a skeptic. What additional information would you want to know when providing your response?

Straight (and Narrow) Talk

Looking again at the reasons given for rejecting Jesus as the only way to God, we find the following flawed thinking:

- *Majority Vote Determines Truth*: There is an old saying that, "What is popular is not always right, and what is right is not always popular." Something can certainly be true whether the majority of people believe it or not. If the majority of Americans agreed that California was the largest state, it would not suddenly make it true. Truth is true regardless of its popularity level.

- *Christianity Is Intolerant*: Is it intolerant to tell people the truth? If there was a fire in a building and a person ran in shouting, "Get out, there's a fire!" would it be reasonable for those in the building to respond, "You are so intolerant. How could you suggest there is a fire in this building?" Christianity claims to be exclusive, but that does not make it intolerant.
- *Hard Work Is Enough*: If Christianity offers heaven as a free gift to those who accept Christ, does that mean that those who work hard are entitled even more? That depends on what level of effort it takes to enter heaven. God said His standard to gain heaven by our own works was perfection in every thought, word, and action. The only reason those who believe in Jesus are able to enter is because of the free gift of God's salvation by His grace through faith. Jesus lived a perfect life on our behalf and paid for all of our sins. All of this is credited to our lives the moment we believe. No level of work, no matter how sincere, can compensate.
- *The Bible Is Lying*: The Bible claims to be a perfect book. Either it is or it is not. However, those who use this excuse have often never even taken time to seriously seek the evidence regarding the Bible's accuracy and integrity. This is often simply an accusation to avoid accepting what the Bible says. (See our Contenders™ study *How Do We Know the Bible Is True?* for more on this issue.)
- *Nice People Go to Heaven*: Do all "nice" people go to heaven? That's not what the Bible teaches, nor does it work in many other places. For instance, I can walk into a bank and ask for money, acting as nice as humanly possible, but I will not be given a penny if I don't have an established account. "Nice" does not replace membership. A person still has to have

access. With God, that "access" is granted through a relationship with Jesus Christ, the one He sent to Earth for this very purpose.

7. Which of the above bullet points makes the most sense to you? Which area is the most difficult to accept?

8. In what other ways do you see these issues at work in the world around you today, perhaps at work or in your school?

9. In what ways do people in today's churches often follow the flawed thinking listed above to some degree? Which area of flawed thinking have you seen the most within church settings?

What to Do with Jesus?

There are only so many conclusions a person can reach when it comes to the claims of Jesus. Here are the four options each person must select from for his or her own life today:

Legend	Jesus didn't even exist.
Lunatic	Jesus was sincere, but sincerely wrong.
Liar	Jesus intentionally misled people.
Lord	Jesus spoke the truth. He is the Christ.

Which option makes the most sense? Historically, there are more known facts regarding Jesus that many other figures in ancient history. If He was out of His mind, then why were the people amazed at His teachings? How was it possible for His followers to reach people around the world teaching those same beliefs? If He was a liar, when and in what way did he lie? Can any of His recorded statements be proven wrong or inaccurate? But what if He is the Lord? Then how should we respond? We would rightly respond by doing what He taught, which includes following what He said regarding entrance into heaven.

10. Do you think the possible views of Jesus can all fit within the four choices listed above? If not, what other options would you suggest? Which option seems the most reasonable?

11. People often refer to Jesus as a good moral teacher, yet will not consider Him as God's Son. In what ways is this approach inconsistent?

SESSION 5

What Now?

12. In what ways does suggesting there is more than one way to heaven belittle what Jesus did on the cross?

13. If Jesus is really the only way to heaven, what implications does this have for your own life today?

14. If Jesus is the only way to heaven, then what does this mean regarding how you share this information with others?

Consider This

Select a statement from each category that best represents what you believe as a result of this discussion:

15. Regarding heaven:
    ___ There is more than one way to enter heaven.
    ___ There is only one way to enter heaven—through Jesus.
    ___ Everyone goes to heaven.
    ___ No one goes to heaven.
    ___ I'm not sure what I believe about heaven.

16. Regarding Jesus:

___ Jesus was just a good teacher.

___ Jesus is God's Son and the only way to heaven.

___ Jesus never existed (or there is no way to know He existed).

___ Jesus was an inaccurate teacher, whether sincerely or insincerely.

___ I'm not sure what I think about Jesus.

17. If Jesus is the only way:

___ I need to place my faith in Him, but let others choose whatever they want. There is no need to attempt to change the beliefs of others.

___ I need to place my faith in Him and help others do the same.

___ I'm not sure what this means for me right now.

What about People Who Haven't Heard of Jesus?

Shawn arrived at his office desk just as the clock struck nine o'clock. His manager walked over and mentioned, "Shawn, I need that JSA report in five minutes."

"What report?" Shawn asked. "You never mentioned it."

"Well, I need it anyway. Just do it."

Frantically, Shawn searched his computer files for anything related to his manager's request. However, nothing matched. He picked up the phone and dialed his manager's extension.

"How can you ask me for a report I have no information on? Where am I supposed to find this stuff?"

His manager scoffed. "I'm the one in charge around here. Don't question me on this."

The next sound Shawn heard was the click on the receiver as the call ended.

"How unfair!" Shawn muttered to himself. "How can he hold me responsible for information he never told me? What kind of leader does he think he is, anyway?"

Is this how God relates with people today? Why would He make people responsible for information they have never heard? If Jesus is so important, why hasn't God created some way for everyone in the world to have a fair shot at hearing about it and having an equal choice?

What about those people who are very religious, yet follow a different god than Christians follow? Is this such a serious "sin" that God would send them to hell for eternity? Aren't these circumstances beyond their control? Can people really be held responsible just because they were born in another culture or into a different religion? What about infants who die, people who are mentally unable to make such choices, or those people who have never even heard that there is a Jesus? Will they all be sent to some fiery hell, too? What kind of God would do that? It doesn't sound like a very loving or fair way to function.

But if Christianity really is exclusive and open only to those who specifically believe in Christ, then isn't that the conclusion? It appears that the very God who claims to be so caring is really turning His back on large numbers of people. What happens to those who have never heard about Jesus?

Talk about It

1. Share about a time when you were asked to do something when you had no idea how to do it. What happened?

2. What are some of your questions regarding people who have never heard about Jesus?

3. Do you think God holds people responsible for what they do not know about Him? Why or why not?

4. What if everyone who had not heard about Jesus was granted automatic entry into heaven. What motivation would missionaries have to travel to other cultures to expose innocent people to Jesus if it would put the people they share with at risk of going to hell if they rejected it?

Here's What I'm Thinking

Are Those Who Haven't Heard about Jesus Innocent?

The Bible clearly indicates that people who live in areas where they have not heard about Jesus are far from innocent:

> Surely *I was sinful at birth*, sinful from the time my mother conceived me. (Psalm 51:5)

SESSION 6

*Therefore, just as sin entered the world through one man, and death through sin, and in this way death came to all men, because **all sinned.** . . .* (Romans 5:12)

*For since the creation of the world God's invisible qualities—his eternal power and divine nature—have been clearly seen, being understood from what has been made, so that **men are without excuse.*** (Romans 1:20)

According to the Bible, every person on the planet is a person who was born with a sinful nature, commits specific wrongful acts of varying degrees, and therefore requires the forgiveness and salvation available only through Jesus Christ. Why would Jesus teach us to "make disciples of all nations" (Matthew 28:19) if people around the world did not need the solution that only Jesus provides? If those who have not heard are innocent, then they don't need to hear. But because all people have sinned, all people need to hear the message that can provide an answer to their sins.

5. Do you agree that those who have not heard about Jesus are in desperate need of Him? Why or why not?

6. If God is perfect in every way, would He allow those who have not heard about Jesus to die and go to hell? How could God be considered loving for doing this?

Is It Fair to Condemn Those Who Have Not Heard?

Yes, God is just to condemn those who have never received His special revelation. First, through general revelation they know about God's "eternal power and Godhead" (Romans 1:20). They are aware that he "made heaven and earth and sea and everything in them" (Acts 14:15). They are aware that God "has not left himself without testimony: he has shown kindness by giving you rain from heaven and crops in their seasons" (Acts 14:17). Although they do not have the Law of Moses, "All who sin apart from the law will also perish apart from the law. . . . Indeed, when Gentiles, who do not have the law, do by nature things required by the law, they are a law for themselves, even though they do not have the law [of Moses], since they show that *the requirements of the law are written on their hearts* (Romans 2:12–15).

Even though God has revealed Himself to all people in creation through their conscience, fallen humanity has universally rejected that light. Hence, God is not obligated to give them any more light, since they have turned from the light they have. In fact, although they have the truth, "the wrath of God is being revealed from heaven against all the godlessness and wickedness of men who suppress the truth by their wickedness" (Romans 1:18). Someone lost in the darkness of a dense jungle that sees one speck of light should go toward it. If that person turns away from the little light and becomes forever lost in darkness, there is only one person to blame. The Scriptures say, "This is the verdict: Light has come into the world, but men loved darkness instead of light because their deeds were evil" (John 3:19).

If any unbeliever truly sought God as a result of following general revelation, God provided the special revelation sufficient for salvation. After God led Peter to the Gentile Cornelius, Peter declared: "I now realize how true it is that God does not show favoritism but accepts men from every nation who fear him and do what is right" (Acts 10:35). The writer of Hebrews tells us that those who seek, find; "he rewards those who earnestly seek him" (Hebrews 11:6).

God has many ways at his disposal through which He can get the truth of the gospel to lost souls. The usual way is through preachers of the gospel (Romans 10:14–15), whether in person or media such as radio, TV, internet, or other technology. On a future occasion God will use an angel to preach the gospel "to every nation, tribe, language and people" (Revelation 14:6). Many people have been given a Bible, read it, and been saved. Others have been saved through gospel literature. We have no way of knowing whether God has conveyed special revelation through visions, dreams, and in other miraculous ways. The truth is that God is more willing that all be saved than we are. "The Lord is not slow in keeping his promise, as some understand slowness. He is patient with you, not wanting anyone to perish, but everyone to come to repentance" (2 Peter 3:9). God's justice demands that He condemn all sinners, but His love compels Him to provide salvation for all who by His grace will believe: "Everyone who calls on the name of the Lord will be saved" (Romans 10:13).

One thing is important to keep in mind. To send people to hell who have never heard is not unjust. To think so is like claiming that it is not right for someone to die of a disease for which there is a cure of which he or she has not yet heard. The crucial question is how one got the disease, not whether he or she has heard of a cure. What is more, if one desires neither to know there is a cure nor to do what is necessary to get cured, then he or she is most certainly culpable.[16]

7. In what ways do you agree or disagree with the above response to those who have not heard?

8. If people know something is wrong according to their conscience and do it anyway, are they guilty of sinning against a holy God? Why or why not? Do they need a remedy or answer for these kinds of sins?

9. What do some of the above verses say about the spiritual knowledge that all people have, regardless of their location or exposure to Jesus?

Those Who Are Unable to Respond

What about those who are unable to respond, such as young children and the mentally challenged? Though it is difficult from the Bible to give exact answers on this issue, the following guidelines help us understand God's position on the issue:

- *God is perfect and His ways are perfect*: "He is the Rock, his works are perfect, and all his ways are just. A faithful God who does no wrong, upright and just is he" (Deuteronomy 32:4). He will ultimately do what is best for those who are unable to make a decision for themselves.
- *All people are sinners and are in need of God's grace for salvation*: "For all have sinned, and fall

short of the glory of God" (Romans 3:23). Every
person is born with a sinful nature and requires
God's grace to produce change. For those who are
unable to respond to enter heaven, God must provide
the grace for it.

This being the situation, it is often concluded that God's grace
extends through Christ's payment for sins to provide for those
who are unable to respond by faith, either because they are
too young to choose or are mentally incapable of making a
choice.

A biblical example of this is found in the life of King
David. The son that was born to him through his affair with
Bathsheba lived for seven days of sickness, during which time
David fasted, wept, and prayed for him. After it was reported
to David that his newborn son had died:

> Then David got up from the ground. After he
> had washed, put on lotions and changed his
> clothes, he went into the house of the LORD
> and worshiped. Then he went to his own
> house, and at his request they served him
> food, and he ate.
>
> His servants asked him, "Why are you acting
> this way? While the child was alive, you
> fasted and wept, but now that the child is
> dead, you get up and eat!"
>
> He answered, "While the child was still alive,
> I fasted and wept. I thought, 'Who knows?
> The LORD may be gracious to me and let
> the child live.' But now that he is dead, why
> should I fast? Can I bring him back again? *I
> will go to him, but he will not return to me.*"
> (2 Samuel 12:20–23)

In this case, David notes that he (David) will go to where his son is. Where would David go? To heaven. Hebrews 11:32–40 later indicates that David was commended for his faith, meaning he went to heaven upon death. The Bible here shows us that children who die do go to heaven, though we are not given a specific age when this would change.

10. What have you traditionally been told about what happens to young children and people who are mentally challenged after death? In what ways have these answers been helpful or unhelpful to you?

11. In Isaiah 55:8–9, God says, "For my thoughts are not your thoughts, neither are your ways my ways. . . . As the heavens are higher than the earth, so are my ways higher than your ways and my thoughts than your thoughts." How could these words apply to the question concerning young children and the mentally challenged who die and enter heaven?

What Now?

12. What are some reasons why people would not want to believe that God allows those who have not heard about Jesus to go to hell?

13. What are the implications for us if we accept the biblical teaching that those who do not hear about Jesus will go to hell? How does this personally motivate you to do something to help reach the unreached?

Consider This

Mark all that apply from the following statements:

14. I believe that:
    ___ Everyone goes to heaven.
    ___ Some people will go to heaven even if they have never heard of Jesus.
    ___ Those who believe in Jesus Christ will go to heaven, but not those who have not heard about Him.
    ___ I'm still not sure what I believe about those who haven't heard.

15. Since the Bible teaches that those who do not believe on Jesus will go to hell, I desire to...

___ put all of my faith in Jesus and ask Him to enter my life and forgive my sins.

___ help reach the unreached through prayer and financial giving.

___ help other Christians I know to realize the importance of reaching unreached people.

___ further investigate ways I could personally serve in reaching other people groups, possibly even as a missionary.

End your final session in a brief time of silent prayer regarding your next step in your spiritual journey. Afterwards, decide as a group what to do next in your desire to continue your spiritual growth.

Also, don't forget to look at the "Additional Resources" section for audio, videos, internet materials, and books on this issue that can be used personally or as additional group learning tools. In addition, we have provided two appendices for your reference. The first is for those who would like to begin a relationship with God. The second is an outline of Bible verses to help you in praying for other people who have yet to experience the joy of a personal relationship with Christ.

Finally, please have a representative from your group take a moment to send an email via the Contenders series website (www.contendersseries.com) to share highlights from your group with others. We would appreciate any stories of life-change that can be used to encourage others in their spiritual journey. God bless you as you continue growing in your spiritual journey!

SESSION 6

How to Begin a Personal Relationship with God

If you would like to begin a personal relationship with God that promises joy, forgiveness, and eternal life, you can do so right now by doing the following:

1. Believe that God exists and that He sent His Son Jesus Christ in human form to Earth (John 3:16; Romans 10:9).
2. Accept God's free gift of new life through the death and resurrection of God's only son, Jesus Christ (Ephesians 2:8–9).
3. Commit to following God's plan for your life (1 Peter 1:21–23; Ephesians 2:1–7).
4. Determine to make Jesus Christ the ultimate leader and final authority of your life (Matthew 7:21–27; 1 John 4:15).

There is no magic formula or special prayer to begin your relationship with God. However, the following prayer is one that can be used to accept God's free gift of salvation through Jesus Christ by faith:

> "Dear Lord Jesus, I admit that I have
> sinned. I know I cannot save myself. Thank
> You for dying on the cross and taking my
> place. I believe that Your death was for me
> and receive Your sacrifice on my behalf. I
> transfer all of my trust from myself and turn
> all of my desires over to You. I open the door
> of my life to You and by faith receive You as
> my Savior and Lord, making You the ultimate
> Leader of my life. Thank You for forgiving
> my sins and giving me eternal life. Amen."

If you have made this decision, congratulations! You have just made the greatest commitment of your life. As a new follower of Jesus, you will have many questions, and this group is a great place to begin. Let your group leaders know about your decision and ask what resources they have available to assist you in your new spiritual adventure.

Other ways you can grow in your new relationship with God include:

- spending regular time in prayer and Bible reading.
- finding a Bible-teaching church where you can grow with other followers of Christ.
- seeking opportunities to tell others about Jesus through acts of service and everyday conversations.

For more information on growing in your relationship with God, please see www.contendersseries.com or www.johnankerberg.org. You can also receive additional materials by contacting the authors at:

The Ankerberg Theological Research Institute
P.O. Box 8977
Chattanooga, TN 37414
Phone: (423) 892-7722

APPENDIX B:

Praying for Those Who Do Not Believe

The Scriptures provide several ways for us to pray for those who do not know Jesus. However, it's often a daunting task to choose where to begin in praying for others. The following outline of verses is designed to assist in offering biblical prayers for those who do not believe.

1. Pray for God to draw the person to Himself.

   No one can come to me unless the Father who sent me draws him. (John 6:44)

2. Pray that the person would desire God.

   But in their distress they turned to the LORD, the God of Israel, and sought him, and he was found by them. (2 Chronicles 15:4)

   God did this so that men would seek him and perhaps reach out for him and find him, though he is not far from each one of us. (Acts 17:27)

3. Pray for an understanding and acceptance of God's Word.

   Consequently, faith comes from hearing the message, and the message is heard through the word of Christ. (Romans 10:17)

   And we also thank God continually because, when you received the word of God, which you heard from us, you accepted it not as the word of men, but as it actually is, the word of God, which is at work in you who believe. (1 Thessalonians 2:13)

4. Pray that Satan would not blind them.

   When anyone hears the message about the kingdom and does not understand it, the evil one comes and snatches away what was sown in his heart. (Matthew 13:19)

   The god of this age has blinded the minds of unbelievers, so that they cannot see the light of the gospel of the glory of Christ, who is the image of God. (2 Corinthians 4:4)

5. Pray that the Holy Spirit would convict of sin.

   When he comes, he will convict the world of guilt in regard to sin and righteousness and judgment. (Matthew 16:8)

6. Pray for someone to share Christ with them.

   Ask the Lord of the harvest, therefore, to send out workers into his harvest field. (Matthew 9:38)

7. Pray that God provides His grace and repentance. (Repentance is a change of mind that leads to changed behavior.)

*Repent, then, and turn to God, so that your sins
may be wiped out, that times of refreshing may come
from the Lord.* (Acts 3:19)

*For it is by grace you have been saved, through
faith—and this not from yourselves, it is the gift
of God—not by works, so that no one can boast.*
(Ephesians 2:8–9)

8. Pray that they believe and entrust themselves in Jesus
    as Savior.

    *Yet to all who received him, to those who believed
    in his name, he gave the right to become children of
    God.* (John 1:12)

    *I tell you the truth, whoever hears my word and
    believes him who sent me has eternal life and will
    not be condemned; he has crossed over from death
    to life.* (John 5:24)

9. Pray that they confess Jesus as Lord.

    *That if you confess with your mouth, "Jesus is
    Lord," and believe in your heart that God raised him
    from the dead, you will be saved. For it is with your
    heart that you believe and are justified, and it is with
    your mouth that you confess and are saved.* (Romans
    10:9–10)

10. Pray that they continue to grow spiritually and learn
    how to surrender all to follow Jesus.

    *Then Jesus said to his disciples, "If anyone would
    come after me, he must deny himself and take up his
    cross and follow me."* (Matthew 16:24)

    *"But whatever was to my profit I now consider
    loss for the sake of Christ. What is more, I consider*

everything a loss compared to the surpassing greatness of knowing Christ Jesus my Lord, for whose sake I have lost all things. I consider them rubbish, that I may gain Christ. (Philippians 3:7–8)

So then, just as you received Christ Jesus as Lord, continue to live in him, rooted and built up in him, strengthened in the faith as you were taught, and overflowing with thankfulness. (Colossians 2:6–7)

Additional Resources

Interested in learning more? For those seriously pursuing more on the life of Christ and Christianity, several additional quality tools exist. We have listed below several other resources available from The Ankerberg Theological Research Institute along with a list of helpful websites on the subject.

Ankerberg Theological Research Institute Resources

All of the following Ankerberg resources can be ordered online at www.johnankerberg.org or by phone at (423) 892–7722.

Books

All of the following books are authored or coauthored by Dr. John Ankerberg or Dillon Burroughs:

Comparing Christianity with the Cults (Chicago, IL: Moody, 2007).

Comparing Christianity with World Religions (Chicago, IL: Moody, 2007).

Defending Your Faith (Chattanooga, TN: AMG Publishers, 2007). (Following God Bible Study Series).

Encyclopedia of New Age Beliefs (Eugene, OR: Harvest House, 1996).

The Facts on Hinduism (Eugene, OR: Harvest House, 1991).

The Facts on Islam (Eugene, OR: Harvest House, 1991).

The Facts on Jehovah's Witnesses (Eugene, OR: Harvest House, 2003).

The Facts on the Mormon Church (Eugene, OR: Harvest House, 2003).

The Facts on World Religions (Eugene, OR: Harvest House, 2004).

Fast Facts on Defending Your Faith (Eugene, OR: Harvest House, 2002).

Fast Facts on Jehovah's Witnesses (Eugene, OR: Harvest House, 2003).

Fast Facts on Mormonism (Eugene, OR: Harvest House, 2003).

Fast Facts on Islam (Eugene, OR: Harvest House, 2001).

Ready with An Answer for the Tough Questions About God (Eugene, OR: Harvest House, 1997).

What's the Big Deal About Other Religions? (Eugene, OR: Harvest House, 2007).

Video and Audio Programs & Transcripts

The following topics are available in VHS & DVD format. Most programs offer downloadable transcripts as well.

105 Years in the Watchtower Service (Jehovah's Witnesses)

Eight Christian Scholars Defend the Faith and Answer Difficult Questions

Ex-Jehovah's Witnesses Convention

Former Jehovah's Witnesses Testify

Former Muslims Testify About Islam

Has The Watchtower Ever Lied, Covered Up, or Changed Important Doctrines, Dates, and Biblical Interpretations? (Jehovah's Witnesses)

How You Can Lead a Jehovah's Witness to Faith in Jesus Christ

How to Witness to a Jehovah's Witness

Interview with Dr. Walter Martin on Cults

Is Islam Opposed to Democracy and Christianity?

Islam and Christianity

Jehovah's Witnesses Distortions Concerning the Deity of Jesus Christ

Jesus, Salvation and the Bible: What do Mormons and Jehovah's Witnesses Believe?

What Do Muslims Believe?

What Islam Teaches About: Jesus' Return, Armageddon, Jerusalem and the Jews

What You Need to Know When Jehovah's Witnesses Come Knocking at Your Door

Where Is Islam Taking the World?

Online Articles

Over 2,500 online articles on Christianity and comparative religions are hosted on The Ankerberg Theological Research Institute website. For an A to Z directory, see http://www. johnankerberg.org/Articles/archives-ap.htm.

About the Authors

Dr. John Ankerberg is host of the award-winning apologetics TV and radio program *The John Ankerberg Show*, which is broadcast in more than 185 countries. Founder and president of the Ankerberg Theological Research Institute, John has authored more than sixty books, including the bestselling *Facts On* apologetics series, with over 2 million copies in print, and *Defending Your Faith* (AMG Publishers). His training includes three earned degrees: a Master of Arts in church history and the philosophy of Christian thought, a Master of Divinity from Trinity Evangelical Divinity School, and a Doctor of Ministry from Luther Rice Seminary. For more information, see www.johnankerberg.org.

Dillon Burroughs is a research associate for the Ankerberg Theological Research Institute. Author or coauthor of numerous books, including *Defending Your Faith* (AMG Publishers), *What's the Big Deal About Jesus?*, and *Comparing Christianity with World Religions*, Dillon is a graduate of Dallas Theological Seminary and lives in Tennessee with his wife, Deborah, and two children.

Endnotes

1   These guidelines adapted from Judson Poling, *How Reliable Is the Bible?*, rev. ed., (Grand Rapids, MI: Zondervan, 2003), pp. 14-15.

2   Larry King Live interview on February 16, 2006. Accessed at http://www.celebatheists.com/index.php?title=George_Clooney.

3   Cited in http://www.afajournal.org/2006/october/1006church. asp.

4   Cited at http://www.leaderu.com/wri/articles/paths.html.

5   Kenneth Richard Samples, "Do All Religions Lead to God?" *Facts of Faith*, Issue 8, 2002. Accessed at http://www.reasons.org/resources/fff/2002issue08/index.shtml.

6   Norman Geisler in *Who Made God?* Ravi Zacharias and Norman Geisler, eds. (Grand Rapids, MI: Zondervan, 2003), pp. 138-139.

7   Adapted from Vincent McCann, "Are All Religions More or Less the Same?" Spotlight Ministries, 2000. Accessed at http://www.spotlightministries.org.uk/plural.htm.

8   Barry Schwartz, "Too Many Choices," *AARP Bulletin*, April 2005. Accessed at http://www.aarp.org/bulletin/yourlife/many_choices. html.

9   Tori DeAngelis, "Too Many Choices?" *APA Online Monitor*, June 2004. Accessed at http://www.apa.org/monitor/jun04/toomany.html.

10   Harold A. Netland, *Dissonant Voices* (Grand Rapids, MI: Eerdmans, 1991), p. 37.

11   Some of this material is adapted from Steven Cory and Dillon Burroughs, *Comparing Christianity with World Religions* (Chicago, IL: Moody, 2007).

12   Steve Russo, "Don't All Spiritual Paths Lead to God?" *Breakaway Magazine*, 2005. Accessed at http://www.breakawaymag. com/GodFaith/A000000013.cfm.

13   These examples adapted from Robert Morey, *How to Keep Your Faith While in College* (Southbridge, MA: Crowne Publications, 1989).

14   Gerald C. McDermott, *Can Evangelicals Learn from Other Religions?* (Downers Grove, IL: Intervarsity Press, 2000), p. 216.

15   "Mormon Growth Rate Rises," *The Watchman Expositor*, 2000. Accessed at http://www.watchman.org/expo/15_3news.htm.

16   Adapted from the Ankerberg Theological Research Institute article "Salvation of the 'Heathen,' " by Dr. Norman Geisler. Accessed at http://www.johnankerberg.org/Articles/Salvation/Salvation%20PDF/ salvation-heathen.pdf.

CONTENDERS BIBLE STUDY SERIES

Questions about God, Christianity, and the Bible aren't going away. How will you respond?

The challenging uncertainties in your mind, or in the mind of someone you know, are worth taking time to explore. In six engaging sessions designed to get small groups talking, each guide in the Contenders Bible Study Series™ deals head-on with some of the controversies commonly asked about Christianity.

How Do We Know God Exists?
(ISBN-13: 978-089957781-4) 5.5" x 8.5"
Paperback / 112 pages

Why Does God Allow Suffering and Evil?
(ISBN-13: 978-089957782-1) 5.5" x 8.5"
Paperback / 112 pages

How Do We Know the Bible Is True?
(ISBN-13: 978-089957779-1) 5.5" x 8.5"
Paperback / 112 pages

How Is Christianity Different from Other Religions?
(ISBN-13: 978-089957780-7) 5.5" x 8.5"
Paperback / 112 pages

Call 800-266-4977 to order
or log on to www.amgpublishers.com